KU-672-356

BEIJING

BEIJING

Photography by Magnus Bartlett, Anthony Cassidy,
China Photo Library, Pat Lam, Joan Law, Leong Ka Tai,
James Montgomery, Ingrid Morejohn,
William Ng (The Stock House), Basil Pao,
Jacky Yip (China Photo Library),
Wan Yat Sha (Shuttle Production) and Carolyn Watts

Text by May Holdsworth

HARRAP COLUMBUS

Copyright © 1988, The Guidebook Company Limited,
Hong Kong

All rights reserved. No part of this publication may be
reproduced or transmitted in any form or by any
means, electronic or mechanical, including photocopy,
recording or any information storage and retrieval
system, without permission from the publisher.

Published by Harrap Limited
19—23 Ludgate Hill, London EC4M 7PD
and The Guidebook Company Limited
The Penthouse, 20 Hollywood Road
Central, Hong Kong

Text and captions by May Holdsworth

Photography by Magnus Bartlett (19 top, 29, 40—41,
46 bottom right, 48); Anthony Cassidy (20 bottom,
64 bottom); China Photo Library (8—9); Pat Lam (73);
Joan Law (12—13, 18 bottom, 19 bottom, 28 left/right
top two, 34 top/bottom, 56, 58 left/top right/bottom
right, 60, 61 top/bottom, 68 right, second from bottom);
Leong Ka Tai (6—7, 14—15, 23, 62, 63, 66, 68 left, 69,
70, 71); James Montgomery (2—3, 24—25 top/bottom left,
42, 43, 46 left, 51 right, 57); Ingrid Morejohn (20 centre,
22 top, 44 top/bottom, 45, 46 top, 47, 53); William Ng,
The Stock House (54—55); Basil Pao (20 top, 21, 30—31,
32—33, 37 bottom, 39, 64 top, 67, 68 right top two/
bottom, 72, 74, 75, 76, 77); Shuttle Production (5, 10—11,
26—27, 38, 49, 50—51 left, 78—79); Jacky Yip, China
Photo Library (18 top, 22 bottom, 25 bottom right,
37 top, 59); Carolyn Watts (35, 58 middle right, 65 top/
bottom).

1	2	3
	4	5	6
7	8	9
10	11	14
12	13	

Page 36:
James Montgomery 1, 10;
Ingrid Morejohn 3, 4, 7, 8;
Joan Law 2, 5, 6, 9; Basil
Pao 12, 13; Jacky Yip,
China Photo Library 11, 14.

Designed by Joan Law Design & Photography
Colour separations by Rainbow Graphic Arts Co., Ltd.
Printed in Hong Kong

ISBN: 0-7471-0118-3

Title spread
*The Hall of Prayer for Good
Harvests at the Temple of
Heaven is an evocative symbol
of Beijing. In imperial days it
was a shrine for annual rites.
The very structure of the hall is
endowed with mystic features.
Its triple-tiered roof, for example,
is covered in celestial blue tiles
and capped with a golden orb.
Inside, the roofs are supported
by 28 pillars: the four central
columns represent the seasons,
while two circles of 12 pillars
stand for the months of the year
and the double-hour periods of
the day.*

Right
*Gilded bosses on a door handle
at Yikungong, one of the six
inner western palaces
traditionally occupied by
imperial concubines. Emperors'
wives were ranked in ascending
levels of importance and favour.
During the Qing Dynasty there
were, from the empress
downwards, eight grades of
imperial consorts.*

Pages 6-7
*The Chinese call it 'Wanli
Changcheng', the Long Wall of
Ten-Thousand Miles. For many
travellers the Great Wall is the
most exciting sight of all the
extant ancient structures in
China. No-one fails to marvel at
the fact that this stupendous
bulwark of stone, twisting like a
dragon across apparently
inaccessible country, is the
work of man. Stretches of the
wall followed the lines of
fortifications that were erected
from the fifth century BC
onwards. Under the First
Emperor, who unified China in
221 BC, a continuous wall was
completed by linking up the
existing fortifications.*

Pages 8-9
Beihai Park.

Page 10-11
*This sumptuously decorated
ceiling is one of many equally
ornate examples to be found in
the halls of the Imperial Palace.
Dragons and clouds, signifying
power and heaven, are imperial
motifs which adorned the
buildings, furniture and robes of
emperors.*

Pages 12-13
*Five marble bridges with carved
balustrades span the Golden
Stream in front of the first
throne hall of the Imperial
Palace.*

Pages 14-15
*Despite the cold, the people of
Beijing throng the New Year fair
at the Temple of Earth Park.*

U.S.S.R.

Mongolia

Urümqi
Turpan

Kashgar

Inner Mongolia

Hetian

Dunhuang
Anxi
Jiayuguan

Yellow River

Hohhot

Beijing

Tianjin

SEA
OF
JAPAN

North Korea

South Korea

Great Wall

Nanjing

Tibet

Lanzhou

Luoyang

Grand Canal

YELLOW
SEA

Shigatse

Xi'an

Lhasa

Shanghai
Suzhou

Hangzhou

Yangzi River

EAST
CHINA
SEA

Kunming

Guilin

Taiwan

Nanning

Macau

Guangzhou

Hong Kong

CHINA

INTRODUCTION

THE FIRST THING that strikes the visitor to Beijing, as he sweeps along the great avenue from the airport, is that the landscape of China's capital is being modernized. It is true that in terms of the preponderance of highrises, the metropolis still lags behind the capitals of the West. Nevertheless, confronted by multi-storey housing blocks that appear so drab and utilitarian, and the highways and flyovers that loop and weave between them, the visitor is understandably dismayed that first impressions of the capital appear so remote from his imagined picture of the heart of an ancient civilization. He has not, after all, come to Beijing to look at the landmarks of contemporary urban construction. Yet for anyone prepared to delve a little into China's history, the glories of Beijing remain accessible through some of the most spectacular monuments ever built.

Chinese guidebooks to Beijing invariably begin with a history of settlement and development. They will tell you that, as the bones of 'Peking Man' attest, the site near Beijing now known as Zhoukoudian was inhabited in prehistoric times. A leap of several hundred thousand years takes this history to the ascendancy of the northern Kingdom of Yan in the 11th century BC. The Kingdom of Yan established its capital, Yanjing, southwest of present-day Beijing. The Liao Dynasty, founded in AD 947 by the Khitan (a Mongolian tribe), chose the same site for their secondary capital, which they renamed Nanjing. Thereafter the Jurchens (Golden Tartars), the Mongols, the founders of the Ming, and finally the Manchus came and conquered. They called their principal city by various names — Zhongdu (the Central Capital), Dadu (the Great Capital), Beiping (Northern Peace) and Beijing (the Northern Capital) — but their palaces were raised on roughly the same site, not far from where primitive cavemen walked 500,000 years ago.

That this history of the city resembles a catalogue of dynasties gives the vital clue to the personality of Beijing. The city has long been the focus of power in the land, never more so than since 1949, when it became the political centre of the world's most populous communist state. But the choice of Beijing as capital over seven centuries reflects another interesting facet of the city's history: unlike Chang'an (Xi'an), Luoyang or Nanjing, the site has been more favoured by alien invaders than by Chinese dynasties.

This is because the area was close to the conquerors' own homelands, being at the northern tip of the North China Plain and within riding distance of the Great Wall passes, through which these nomads launched their raids. The richer and more populous parts of the empire, however, lay farther south, around the fertile delta of the Yangzi River. One of the oldest cities on the river was Nanjing, where the founder of the Ming Dynasty fixed his capital in the second half of the 14th century. Beijing was then renamed Beiping.

The third Ming emperor, Yongle, re-established the capital in Beijing on his usurpation of the throne in 1403. Partly this was because the northeast had been his power base; the move was also made at a time when the militarily strong empire was well able to defend its frontiers against troublesome nomads. It was during this era of peace that the massive building projects in and around Beijing were undertaken. Fortifications and walls went up, the Forbidden City was built, and the great tombs to the north were constructed.

Tiananmen or the Gate of Heavenly Peace, perhaps the most dramatic of paradoxes — evoking both a strong feeling of continuity and, at the same time, an equally powerful sense of change — was also erected then. In the days of empire it spanned the thoroughfare that led to the Forbidden City; now it marks the northern perimeter of the vast square overlooked by a portrait of Chairman Mao. From the rostrum of the Gate of Heavenly Peace Mao Zedong proclaimed the founding of the People's Republic of China in 1949, rather as, in earlier times, emperors issued edicts from the tower of the Meridian Gate, the entrance proper to the Forbidden City. The vast square itself, so assertively an

A portrait of Chairman Mao is the centrepiece of the Gate of Heavenly Peace (Tiananmen). Visitors may now climb to the upper storey of the gate for an uninterrupted view of the huge square to the south. Mao's portrait is flanked by two long plaques inscribed with characters which read: 'Long Live the People's Republic of China' on the left and 'Long Live the Solidarity of the People of the World' on the right.

The Bank of China, at Tiananmen.

example of socialist reconstruction, is a symbol of the triumph of the proletariat — indeed, Tiananmen constitutes the central motif of the national emblem of China. Lately, in the relatively more liberal mood of the nation, the Tiananmen rostrum has been thrown open to any tourist willing to pay the entrance fee for the thrill of being photographed where Chairman Mao once stood and perhaps dreamed of the rebirth of China.

To the contemporary eye the ordinary reality of the city is revealed by the stir of activity that spreads across Tiananmen on a fine day. For an afternoon the square becomes the setting for perhaps a display of potted shrubs, arranged in the contours of a snaking Great Wall; or the backdrop for a family snapshot, taken by one of the several photographers who have set up their stands here to ply their services to out-of-towners; or the preserve of kite-flyers, gently and skilfully letting their paper butterflies and dragons out to the wind.

South of Tiananmen, the Avenue of Eternal Peace (Chang'an Jie) runs east-west and forms part of the centre ring road. One can trace the line of the old inner city wall along its course and capture a sense of the regularity and scale of Ming town planning. On the original rectangular grid later builders have superimposed the wide, straight boulevards — some with as many as six rows of trees — which so strikingly characterize the face of Beijing. These long arterial roads are still traversed by phalanxes of bicycles, the only form of wheels for millions of the inhabitants, for all that Beijing boasts a subway and more passenger motor vehicles than any other city in China except Canton.

Although most of the city gates have been torn down, the names of the main roads still recall their former locations. Fuxingmennei is literally 'Within Revival Gate'; Jianguomenwai means 'Outside Building-Nation Gate'. During the Cultural Revolution anti-reactionary fervour played havoc with street names, but these have now reverted to their pre-1966 originals: the address of the Soviet Embassy, previously Anti-Revisionism Road, is once more North-Central Street of Dongzhi Gate; Eternally Red Street is again, more cosily, Street of Soyabean Sprouts.

Leaving the crowded roads, one passes into the mazes of back alleys, known as *hutongs*, still to be found behind the main thoroughfares. These residential enclaves have been part of the character of Beijing for some six to seven hundred years. The Qing Empress Dowager Cixi is believed to have spent her childhood in one, Xila Hutong, off Wangfujing. Whereas in other regions of China such lanes might be termed *xiang, li, long* or *fang*, the name for Beijing's side streets is derived from Mongolian.

The *hutongs* are also congested, but here the din of traffic and movement of the main avenues softens to a drone of individual voices and the clatter of domestic life. Young and old are crammed into the traditional courtyard dwellings here, living in an intimacy dictated by the severe housing shortage. More desirable accommodation may be increasingly provided by apartment buildings in the suburbs, but in a municipality with more than nine and a half million residents, two-generation households still greatly outnumber those consisting of nuclear families or single people. Behind the tumble-down courtyard walls a host of household possessions, from enamel washbowls and bicycles to bamboo stools and airing bedclothes, overflows from small dark living quarters spartanly furnished with perhaps a table and chairs, and a brazier on which meals are cooked. In warm weather, the routines of daily life are conducted outdoors. Residents cluster at the stone-lintelled doorways to gossip or watch the odd car inching its way along the narrow passage. Groups of elderly men play chess or just huddle together for a companiable smoke under the shade of old elms and willow trees. If there is a local school or crèche, the *hutong* becomes both playing field and gymnasium for brightly attired children ushered into the open for their daily exercise. At the end of the *hutong*, you may find the neighbourhood shops — vegetable, fruit and hardware stalls, the watchmender, cobbler and repairer of umbrellas, kiosks serving steamed buns, scallion pancakes and other filling fare. A greasy, fried dough-cake, which somehow manages to be both sweet and savoury, is widely sold at breakfast time. They can be munched on the way to work, and even foreigners may sometimes try one, if a friendly saleswoman chooses to overlook the requisite grain coupons. The famous Sichuan Restaurant, which Deng Xiaoping has patronized, as proudly witnessed by the photographs hanging in the courtyard, is located in a *hutong*, which is rather trim now that tourists go there in droves.

Fanciful stories have been passed down to account for the phenomenon of *hutongs*. The most amusing one attributes their existence to the fact that Beijing was the capital of a number of dynasties from the 12th century onwards. Whenever the emperor sallied forth from his palace, the roads had to be cleared, for no commoner might look upon the imperial entourage. Any citizen who failed to evacuate the route in time was required to prostrate himself until the procession had passed. The *hutongs*, fanning out from the main avenues, were convenient hiding places in such emergencies.

The area around Jianguomenwai Avenue is the developing business district. China traders march purposefully into the CITIC Building or the Jianguo Hotel, a member of the diplomatic corps crawls through the traffic jam in a sports car (where only a few years ago mules pulling rickety carts sedately clopped), and foreign tourists debouch from coaches at regular intervals to shop at the Friendship Store.

Yet, for all that these sights speak of radical changes to China's economic system, the capital is still pervaded by the ghosts of emperors, concubines and eunuchs. The very grid of the inner city remains that planned by 15th-century Ming geomancers. It is a rectangular network whose straight thoroughfares paralleled and intersected the meridian line, the central north-south axis delineated mathematically from the polar star. Along this axis supreme power flowed from the Dragon Throne.

Even now, the visitor to the Imperial Palace, approaching it through the Meridian Gate, can imagine himself treading the stones of a sacred way, towards the seat of a divine presence. Within the battlemented enclosure, 24 emperors over a period of 500 years performed the rites and functions that were by tradition the prerogatives of priest-kings. Ensconced in the Da Nei (The Great Within) from which they only infrequently emerged, the emperors maintained an aloofness that accentuated their divine aura. The last emperor of China, Puyi, stripped of his throne by the Republicans in 1912 (although he continued to occupy the rear palaces of the Forbidden City until 1924), did not venture beyond the walls of Beijing until 1916, when he was 13 years old.

The brilliant hues of the Forbidden City — the ochre roof ridges of the halls, the mottled red (once likened to the colour of dried blood) of the pavilion facades, the cold white of the marble courtyards — may now be subdued by the layers of unswept sand blown from the Mongolian desert. (A visitor to Beijing in the last century thought the city was all lacquer and gold and dust; a writer in the 1930s said, 'Nowadays there is less lacquer, and less gold, but more dust.') But neither the grime and peeling paint, nor the crowds of sightseers, can exorcize the spirits that hang about these palaces still. Here, in the Palace of Heavenly Purity, the corrupt eunuch Wei Zhongxian, more powerful than the emperor he served, received well-wishers on his birthday. There, in the Palace of Concentrated Beauty, a junior concubine gave birth to a son and was promoted to the First Grade, a rank she subsequently bettered by becoming Regent and ruling China from 'behind a silk screen'. Perhaps this frayed silk curtain is the very same flimsy screen that hid her, while ministers connived at the poignant pretence of reading memorials to their teenage emperor? Did that eastern courtyard well really receive the body of the Pearl Concubine, the tragic victim to Empress Cixi's anger and ambition? Can one almost hear the panting bearers as they carried Puyi on a yellow-tasselled palanquin to his schoolroom across the desolate flagstones? Was it through the Gate of Divine Prowess that Emperor Chongzhen fled, that fateful night in March 1644, to hang himself

The White Dagoba at Beihai Park, built in 1652 in honour of the visit of the Dalai Lama to Beijing, is in the form of a Tibetan reliquary. The shrine crowns an artificial island on Beihai Lake, which was dug in the 12th century, when Beijing was known as Zhongdu.

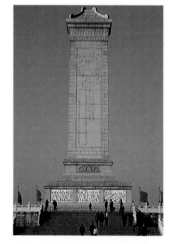

The Monument to the People's Heroes in Tiananmen Square. A granite obelisk of enormous proportions, it is dedicated to the martyrs of the revolution. The gold inscription, composed by Chairman Mao, extols the heroes who laid down their lives in the momentous struggles against 'internal and external enemies' that took place from the Opium War of 1840 to the War of Liberation in the years before 1949.

Children of Beijing.

on Prospect Hill? No empty palace or stately home is so resonant with the echoes of history, even if that history is reduced to a tale of whispered calumnies, subtle punishments and grisly deaths. For all its size and grandeur, the Imperial Palace gives the impression not so much of majesty as of mystery, as though these dark enclosed spaces will yet yield up their secrets.

Tiantan (the Temple of Heaven), now a public park, is best seen at sundown. It hardly matters that the gate to the northern section of the grounds is locked by parkkeepers well before nightfall. From the Bridge of Vermilion Stairs one can see the structures beyond the enclosing wall looming up gracefully above the shadows, and long-winged swifts wheeling around the eaves. The silhouette of the triple conical roof of the Hall of Prayer for Good Harvests, set off by the outlines of the carved marble balustrades, is stunning against a fading light. After the crowds depart, an ancient peace and dignity once more settles over the vast temple area and its lines of sombre cypresses. It is only in an atmosphere of stillness and solemnity that the magic of this beautiful shrine can be appreciated.

From 1420 onwards, emperors came to the temple at the winter solstice to offer sacrifices to *Tian*, or Heaven. To the Chinese, Heaven was the abode of ancestors and the supreme spiritual reality. The emperor's right to rule was believed to be conferred by Heaven, and the continuation of this mandate was dependent upon righteous conduct of the reign. When famine, war and catastrophe visited the land, and rebellions rose up to sweep an emperor from his throne, the usurper could claim the mandate to found a new dynastic line. And historians would vindicate him, since the fallen monarch could always be shown, after the event, to have forfeited the mandate by corrupt rule or immoral behaviour.

The altar here was arguably the holiest shrine in China, for sacrifices at Tiantan could be made only by the Son of Heaven. He alone was the earthly representative of Heaven, possessed of the power to conciliate the gods and enlist their aid for mankind. The emperor would undergo ritual purification for three days before the ceremony, keeping the last night of his vigil at the Hall of Abstinence, a building on one side of the temple complex. In the abattoir the sacrificial offering would be prepared. On the day itself, spirit tablets were taken from the Imperial Vault of Heaven to the marble altar known as the Circular Mound. This is formed by a three-tiered terrace, the top tier of which is made up of a central round flagstone and concentric rings of flagstones arranged in blocks of nine and multiples of nine, mystic numbers in Chinese cosmology. It was upon the central flagstone that the emperor, in resplendent sacrificial robes, worshipped and communed alone with the gods. As he stood under the lightening sky, by a trick of acoustics the sound of his whispers would be bounced back to him by the surrounding balustrades, so that his invocations boomed in his ears. The cold desiccated air of a wintry dawn then filled with smoke as incense burners and horn lanterns were lit, and the sacrificial bull and prayers written on silk were consigned to the flames. Today, tourists from the provinces and abroad cluster on the central flagstone, taking turns to put the curious acoustics to the test.

So powerful a symbol of sovereignty was the annual sacrifice at the Temple of Heaven that, although the pilgrimage in its prescribed form had been discontinued with the Manchu abdication, the ambitious warlord Yuan Shikai, first President of the Republic, re-enacted the ceremony in 1915 to validate his establishment of a new dynasty. This was the last time the ancient rites were performed in Chinese history. But the fact that Yuan made the journey to the temple in an armoured car, and that a photographer was summoned to capture the proceedings on film, robbed the occasion of its customary grandeur and meaning. As for Yuan Shikai's imperial dreams, they barely lasted the month. Bowing to the opposition of anti-monarchists, he postponed and then cancelled his enthronement.

Symmetry marked the town planning of the Ming builders. On either side of the straight north-south road which begins at the heart of the imperial domain, there were once two shrines, for the Temple of Heaven was balanced, on the west, by the Temple of Agriculture. The emperor came to the latter every spring to turn up a few sods with his own hands, a highly significant ritual in a predominantly agricultural realm. The rites, properly performed, ensured the harmony of nature; thus the changing seasons would follow their expected course, land would remain fertile and granaries would be filled.

This measure of a regime's success was central to the Chinese way of thinking and continued to be so even under the communist leadership. The importance placed on self-sufficiency in rice and cereals can be gauged from Mao Zedong's obsession with building grain stocks. In the 1960s he urged, 'Strive for several years so that we shall no longer have to import grain . . . ' and 'dig tunnels deep and store grain everywhere'. Stressing the role of grain production — as fundamental to the economy as industry — the design of the national emblem incorporates, besides the Gate of Heavenly Peace, an ear of wheat and a cogwheel. Unfortunately, a solution to the 'grain problem' eluded Mao in his lifetime, and grain rationing remains a fact of economic life, even if shortages are not apparent in the markets and restaurants of Beijing.

Urban households in Beijing, in common with the majority of city-dwellers elsewhere in China, spend more than half their income on food. Eating is the dominant activity in people's lives, absorbing a sizeable period of the working day. Fast-food used to be anathema to the Chinese, who would no more grab a quick bun in their lunch-break than forego their afternoon siesta. It took two fast-food chefs from Hong Kong, acting as advisors, to introduce the concept of mass-produced convenience meals to Beijing. The citizens have now embraced such innovations as South Xidan Street's Yili, the first Western-style snackbar to be opened in Beijing, and — a latecomer to the city's food scene — Kentucky Fried Chicken. That, as well as pepper steaks, hot dogs and ice cream, has come to stay, alongside salted eggs, deep-fried dough sticks and soyabean milk. Fast-food releases the worker from some domestic chores, but it is still far from displacing home cooking. Housewives may now shop at supermarkets, but they also buy fresh food in the free markets of the city, daily contending with the effects of economic reform in their haggles with vendors over the inflated price of pork and fish.

In December 1987, the Chinese rock star Cui Jian played to enthusiastic fans in Beijing at his first public concert in a year. (Previously he had been banned from performing what to cultural authorities seemed distinctly decadent music.) In the choice of entertainment citizens of the capital are generally more privileged than most Chinese elsewhere in the country, but pop concerts, the theatre and the cinema are not everyday pastimes. Contrast Cui Jian's performance with the following picture of another musical event, one which happens regularly and without the clamour and participation of young Beijingnese: in the early morning, below the White Dagoba in Beihai Park, a handful of elderly opera buffs are singing a favourite aria; perhaps the song is from *The Drunken Beauty*, or *The Fisherman's Revenge*, both well-loved Beijing operas from the traditional repertoire. For the majority of people in Beijing, leisure is represented by such modest diversions, and of course by television and an occasional outing to a scenic spot or famous site. It is to the pavilions, hills and lakes that one should go to join the local people taking their ease. They come on their day off, in couples or family groups. And if their work unit can conjure up a coach, they go farther afield, to enjoy the pastoral pleasures that in a bygone age emperors contrived for themselves.

Yiheyuan has everything for a day's outing. It was the Summer Palace of the Empress Dowager Cixi. There had long been a tradition for the imperial household to escape the hot weather by moving the Court in summer to a country retreat. This one was built for Cixi in celebration of her 60th birthday; it was to be her 'Garden for the

The origins of puppet theatre in China predate written records, but it is thought that the ancient craft may have been associated with ritual magic performed in the course of funereal rites, when effigies were used to stand for the spirit of the dead. The figure shown here is a rod puppet, manipulated from below. Moving such figures is a demanding skill which the puppet master has perfected over many years. In old Beijing many itinerant puppet troupes wandered the city's streets giving performances. The Manchu nobility was particularly fond of puppet shows and had them staged in their houses. Today the Beijing-based National Art Puppet Theatre, consisting of over a hundred puppeteers and musicians, tours the country regularly with popular plays such as Havoc in Heaven.

The Temple of Azure Clouds rises up from terraces cut into a slope of the Western Hills, and the trees (cypress, peach and almond) which surround it enhance the attractions of this lovely site.

The Hall of Prayer for Good Harvests, at the Temple of Heaven. No nails were used in constructing this magnificent wooden structure, and its roofs are supported not by walls but by brackets and pillars.

Harmonious Cultivation of Old Age'. Set along the shores of Kunming Lake, the resort is only 11 kilometres (seven miles) northwest of Beijing. On entering the spacious grounds, one is greeted by the spectacle of pink lotuses framed by velvety green leaves at the edge of the lake. In the middle distance, the Bridge of Seventeen Arches sparkles in the sun. Cixi was fond of going for a row on the still waters, attended by her eunuchs and seemingly oblivious of the miserable fate of her nephew, Emperor Guangxu. For challenging her authority by giving his support to a reform movement, Guangxu spent ten years as Cixi's prisoner in the Hall of Jade Ripples at the southeastern end of the lake. His apartments were later found to be surrounded by brick walls. Nearby, a series of halls linked by covered galleries and courtyards — Cixi's own apartments — leads to a theatre, now restored as a museum. Anyone who shares Cixi's love of theatricals can put on the Qing-Dynasty costumes displayed here and pose for a photograph.

Imperial architects introduced informality to these country residences and sought to enhance nature by digging lakes and building hills. Yiheyuan has both lake and hill, the latter terraced with steps, pavilions and pagodas. The buildings have been taken over by souvenir stores and teashops, but there is no denying their picturesque setting. At the foot of the hill a long covered promenade, its roof and columns floridly painted with vignettes from Chinese folktales and legends, gives an idea of Qing aesthetic taste. The alien Manchus, like other barbarian conquerors before them, came to adopt the superior culture of the defeated race, but their admiration for the art of the past led eventually to endless imitation rather than innovation. The conventional taste of the Manchu Court also can be seen in the style of the numerous curios — overburdened, elaborate and artificial — that are on view at the Summer Palace and the Forbidden City. Examples are the huge cloisonné cranes patterned with coloured enamel; the ornate clocks studded with jewels and inlaid with gold; the carved jadeite *ruyi* (a kind of ornamental sceptre) that looks like a handlebar with bulbous ends; and the heavy lacquer panels covered with marquetry. These artifacts of wealth and opulence made an exaggerated appeal to the senses which helped a dying dynasty to prolong the illusion of its authority.

In 1910 the Dutch scholar Borel said of the city that, 'properly speaking, Peking is all one immense temple, surrounding the recess which is the Forbidden City, where dwells the Deity who is Emperor'. Today the 'New Forbidden City' is at Zhongnanhai, west of the Imperial Palace. This walled area, closed to anyone without security clearance, is occupied by China's present rulers. They too dwell amidst vermilion pillars and latticed windows, and look out over expanses of water fringed by willows. For the villas here were the Central and Southern Lake Palaces of the late Qing Court. Here the Empress Dowager Cixi picnicked and, on a famous occasion, received the ladies of the Foreign Legations; and here, in the early days of the Republic, Yuan Shikai gave his garden parties.

Such echoes from the past remain. For today's traveller to Beijing, to walk through the dusty halls of empty palaces and to wonder at the treasures that fill them is to summon back for an hour or two both the splendour and the decadence of old China.

Right
Pavilion on Kunming Lake, the Summer Palace.

中华人民共和国万岁

Statues guarding the entrance to Mao Zedong's Memorial Hall at Tiananmen. The imposing building was completed in 1977 on the first anniversary of his death. Visitors are allowed to file past the crystal coffin in which the late Chairman's body lies in state.

The Gate of Heavenly Peace is always lit up on May Day, National Day and at the lunar New Year, the three official holidays in the People's Republic.

世界人民大团结万岁

The Great Hall of the People at Tiananmen
is the seat of government. Behind the
granite columns is a vast assembly hall,
where the National People's Congress
convenes, as well as 30 reception rooms for
each province, provincial-level municipality
and autonomous region in China.

Following page
Winter in the Forbidden City.

Left
Entering the Forbidden City. In former times only the emperor used the central opening of the outer triple gates, and the right to proceed to the inner gates on horseback or by sedan chair was conferred as a special privilege upon those officials whom the emperor wished to honour.

Top
Plaque over the door of Qinianmen, at the Temple of Heaven.

Centre and bottom
Doors at the Imperial Palace.

Right
The Gate of Divine Prowess, the Forbidden City.

Above and left
Golden-tiled roofs, sweeping down smoothly in a curve to the eaves, are the most distinctive architectural feature of the palace halls. The style of the curving roofs has been romantically, if not accurately, attributed to an attempt to recreate the outlines of tents.

Pages 30-31
This picture shows the Meridian Gate, the main south gate into the Imperial Palace, from the rear. Among an emperor's ceremonial duties were the reviewing of troops from victorious battles and the issuing of the calendar at New Year. He discharged those duties from the high platform of this massive gate.

Preceding page
Marble bridges over the Golden Stream, with the Gate of Supreme Harmony beyond. Behind the gate lie the three aligned halls of state. The first and also the most monumental is the Hall of Supreme Harmony, the grand audience chamber in which important ceremonies, such as enthronements and New Year celebrations, were conducted.

The immense flagged quadrangles of the Forbidden City divide the principal halls from the inner palaces, which are in turn arranged around courtyards, alleys and gardens, though on a less grandiose plan. By tradition the emperor and his immediate household occupied the three central inner palaces. The later Qing rulers, however, preferred the more intimate eastern and western sections of the inner court and eventually moved their quarters there. Of the eastern palaces, the Palace of Concentrated Beauty and the Palace of Tranquil Longevity are probably the most well known, for they were inhabited by Empress Dowager Cixi. Her successor, Puyi, spent the first decade of the Republic in the western section, having been given permission under the Articles of Favourable Treatment to retain a modest court in the Forbidden City. Most of the rear palaces are now exhibition rooms for some of the countless works of art formerly owned by the imperial family.

Bronze and gilded lions (1, 2 and 7) guard the principal gates within the Forbidden City. Bronze was also used to vigorous effect in the handles of water vats (14) which, together with the sundial (5), cranes, tortoises, grain measures and incense burners, herald the approach to the Hall of Supreme Harmony. The crane and tortoise (9) symbolize longevity. Behind the Hall of Supreme Harmony is the Hall of Central Harmony (11), where the emperor rested before attending ceremonies in the first hall.

The most extensively employed decorative details in the palaces are painted friezes and glazed tilework (3 and 4). The use of rich colour in porcelain tiles, in particular, is a distinctive feature of decorative arts in the Ming Dynasty, when great advances were made in the techniques of glazing and ceramics production. Those techniques, splendidly displayed in the flaring yellow-tiled roofs (6 and 12), may also be seen in the pottery figures that surmount the hips (10). Considered as protectors, such figures took the form of mythical animals and were always grouped in odd numbers.

Shortly after the 1911 revolution, the Forbidden City passed into the hands of the Republicans and was turned into a museum. Today, instead of eunuchs, museum guards stand at the entrances (13). And now that domestic tourism has taken off in China, the Imperial Palace is visited by sightseers from the provinces (8) in increasing numbers.

Top
Imperial Palace wall.

Above
Sightseers in the Forbidden City.

Gate towers at the corners of the Forbidden
City walls. Built in the shape of a pagoda,
these towers contained quarters for guards
on duty and were solid edifices clearly
designed as defensive bastions. The section
of the moat pictured here abuts Beihai
Park.

Following page
Beihai Park seen from Prospect Hill. Located
in the city centre, just northwest of the
Forbidden City, the park is a popular spot
for picnics. Boats hired from the jetty take
visitors across Beihai Lake which, along
with the Central and Southern Lakes or
Zhongnanhai, were the creation of Emperor
Yongle. Prospect Hill also grew out of the
imperial predilection for landscaping; its
five peaks, each crowned by a pavilion,
were reputedly made from earth excavated
when the Forbidden City moat was dug.

Curved around the Imperial Vault of Heaven, the famous Echo Wall is an enduring curiosity for visitors to the Temple of Heaven. They love to stand against the wall to hear their whispers reverberating from a point further along the curve. Memorial tablets — objects of reverence — were stored in the Imperial Vault of Heaven and taken out when the emperor came to the altar for his annual obeisances to Heaven.

The Hall of Prayer for Good Harvests rises from circular terraces of white marble. The wall enclosing it to the north was also built in a curve in the belief that Heaven, where the gods lived, was round.

West of Beijing, at Xizhimenwai, is the site of the 15th-century Five Pagoda Temple. This pagoda, modelled on the Indian Buddhist temple in Bodhgaya, survived the sack of the capital by French and English troops in 1860. Also known as the 'Jewelled Throne', the structure consists of a square platform carved with rows of Buddha images and topped by five small pagodas.

Beautiful bas-relief carvings of Buddhist symbols ornament the sides of the Jewelled Throne and its little pagodas. This one is of Buddha's footprints.

Tibetan Lamaism had a strong following in Beijing in the Qing Dynasty, and the Lama Temple remains a famous sight of the city. Originally the temple was a prince's palace (it is still known as the Yonghegong, the Palace of Harmony and Peace). The prince duly ascended the throne, and since by tradition an emperor's birthplace could never be used as an ordinary residence, the palace became a centre of Buddhist worship. Four languages — Tibetan, Mongolian, Manchu and Chinese — can be discerned on the tablets and plaques of the temple. The inscription shown here is at the Hall of the Wheel of Law.

Left
Astronomical instruments on the rooftop of the Beijing Observatory. When emperors handed down the calendar from the Meridian Gate, they were asserting their authority in a way most directly comprehensible to their subjects. The precision of calendrical calculations in forecasting the succession of the seasons, which made the crucial difference between famine and plenty, reinforced the belief that the emperor was Heaven's messenger. When Jesuit missionaries arrived in China and demonstrated the superiority of European astronomy, they so impressed Emperor Kangxi that he gave them positions at Court. In 1674, celestial globes, theodolites and sextants were made by Father Verbiest for the imperial observatory.

Top two
Decorative detail and a corner of the Summer Palace.

Right
Holiday-makers pose for photographs among the ruins of the Western Mansions at Yuanmingyuan, the old Summer Palace west of Beijing. Reduced to rubble by pillaging Anglo-French troops in 1860, Yuanmingyuan was originally a hunting park filled with palaces and fountains and laid out by Emperor Kangxi, patron of Jesuits. (We know that Kangxi asked Verbiest to build, besides astronomical instruments, 'a water fountain that operated in conjunction with an organ'.) Another Jesuit, Father Castiglione, designed the European-style Western Mansions which were added to the park in 1745.

In contrast to the ruins of Yuanmingyuan, the park which we know as the Summer Palace was restored at great expense after its destruction by European soldiers in 1860. Officially, the palace was presented to Empress Dowager Cixi by her nephew, Emperor Guangxu, as a gesture of devotion and loyalty. At the cost of 700,000 taels of silver, the park was made 'a fitting place for the reception of Our Gracious Sovereign Lady and in celebration of the approaching Joyful Anniversary (her 60th birthday)' in 1888. Her Gracious Sovereign Lady accepted the gift after a suitable show of reluctance.

In an edict the Dowager Empress protested that the costs of rebuilding her Summer Palace were met out of the 'surplus funds accumulated as a result of rigid economies in the past.' In fact the pleasure park was restored with money set aside for expanding China's navy. The Marble Boat, permanently 'moored' on Kunming Lake, was the only addition to the fleet that resulted from Cixi's appropriation of national revenues.

Gilded statues of luohan *(disciples of Buddha) at the Temple of Azure Clouds, which is spread out on a slope of the Fragrant Hills west of Beijing. Each statue is sculpted in a different pose.*

Little remains of the hunting park at the
Fragrant Hills. When first laid out in the
12th century the park abounded in game,
and in the reign of Qianlong the site was
covered with pavilions and temples. The
famous maples, however, still draw visitors
to the wooded slopes, particularly in
autumn when the hillsides are tinted in
copper and gold.

Following page
Cresting mountain tops and clinging to the
slopes, the Great Wall as rebuilt in the Ming
Dynasty meandered for 4,000 kilometres
(2,500 miles) from Liaoning in the east to
Gansu in the west. Parts of the wall, being
constructed of rammed earth, have
disintegrated, but long stretches of it are
still in good condition and several of the
more accessible segments have been
restored. Visitors to Beijing can travel to the
wall at Badaling by train or by road.

Along the parapets, embrasures some two
metres (six feet) high allowed sentries to fire
at invaders. Despite such defences, some of
the nomads whom the Great Wall was
built to keep at bay did manage to break
through the barrier. The most successful
conquerors were the Mongols and
Manchus, who swept down to the fertile
plains of north China and stayed to
establish the Yuan and Qing Dynasties.

The Great Wall cuts through some of the wildest and most remote parts of northern China.

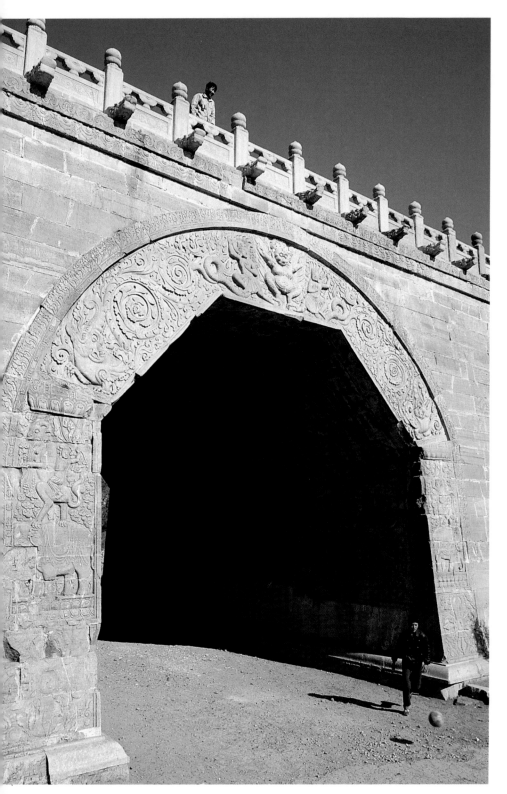

The road from Beijing to the Great Wall at Badaling cuts through Juyong Pass. A fortified village once guarded the passage. All that remains now is this interesting stone gateway, Cloud Terrace (left), which dates from the Yuan Dynasty. No-one knows what function the structure served. It is most remarkable for the carvings over the arch and on its inside walls. Inscriptions etched between the carvings are in six languages — Sanskrit, Tibetan, Mongolian, Uighur, Chinese and Tangut.

Top
It has been said that the top of the Great Wall is so wide that six horses could run abreast along it.

Middle
Where the inclines are particularly steep, the path along the top of the wall is broken by flights of stone steps down which sightseers carefully descend in single file.

Bottom
The most solid segments of the Great Wall were built of earth and rubble faced with brick.

Spaced between half a mile and a mile apart, depending on the terrain, watchtowers punctuate the length of the Great Wall. The watchtowers have an upper observation terrace and a lower storey which accommodated guards or stored ammunition. Beacon towers were also constructed at strategic points along the way. Whenever danger threatened, smoke and fire signals sent from those towers were a remarkably fast and efficient method of putting the faraway capital on the alert. It is said that in very early times, sentries burned wolf dung to make smoke; during the Ming Dynasty, sulphur and saltpetre were also used.

This stone guardian is one of six pairs of statues, representing scholars, officials and warriors, that line Spirit Way to the Ming Tombs. Concealed under artificial hills, the 13 imperial tombs lie scattered in a valley north of Beijing. When opened by archaeologists, Dingling, the tomb of the Wanli Emperor (reigned 1573–1620), was discovered to be filled with treasures. None of the other underground mausoleums in this valley has been excavated.

At the Longtan Park New Year fair, children play around an auspicious dragon and a couple poses with their warmly wrapped baby. The custom of holding New Year fairs, particularly in the bustling environs of city temples, is centuries-old. Nowadays they take place in parks, but are still called 'temple fairs'.

Beijing youngsters at play. Winter in Beijing is and begins around October, when the Siberian anticyclone passes over the Mongolian plateau and moves south. As they gain strength, the winds keep temperatures in Beijing below freezing but they bring little snow. Enough has fallen on Beihai Park, however, for these girls to make a small snowman.

An outing from the Beijing Children's Palace. In most large cities in China there are organized recreation centres known as 'children's palaces' and 'workers' palaces', where facilities for group activities from painting classes to filmshows are provided by the municipal authorities.

Back lot at Beijing Film Studio.
The buildings here are
untouched by modernization, as
are many in Beijing's side alleys.

A tourist from the provinces.

Tiny songbirds make favourite pets in crowded Chinese cities. Keeping pet birds is traditionally regarded as a fitting pastime for retired men and involves nothing more strenuous than taking the birds out for a daily airing. A leafy perch for the cage can usually be found under a willow growing out of a nearby courtyard or, better still, in a park.

Bird market near Guanyuan Park.

鲜果品

Since China launched her economic reforms, free markets have become a familiar sight. They offer the shopper a degree of choice previously unavailable in state-controlled outlets, but they have also encouraged such abuses as the stockpiling of scarce commodities by vendors in order to force up prices.

Despite much higher prices than in state-run shops, better-quality groceries and fresh food in the free markets are always in demand. These people have arrived early to make sure they have the pick of the vegetables offered for sale that morning.

A bustling street (left) contrasts with the near-empty pavement where newspapers and official notices, posted behind glass, fail to draw many passersby (above bottom). A magazine kiosk (second from top) offers a more varied choice of reading matter, from journals on child care to paperback romances. Other side-street services include tailoring (second from bottom). Many such privately run, small-scale enterprises, offering a range of services needed by the community, have flourished in recent years.

In the old days, New Year fairs were never complete without some form of popular theatre such as acrobatics or story-telling. Combining rhymed ballads, narrative, dramatic gestures and facial expressions, the art of story-telling has persisted, although nowadays it is more often performed as part of an indoor variety show than on the street. This story-teller has, however, set up his stage in the open air. He provides his own accompaniment.

One of the happier effects of modernization
in China is a renewed interest in glamour.
City hairdressers and beauty salons are
doing very brisk business now that
permanent waves and makeup are no
longer considered bourgeois and decadent.

A bold poster advertises a retrospective of Yves St Laurent fashions. This exhibition did not lead to the opening of Rive Gauche boutiques in Beijing, but clothes-consciousness has made a comeback in China along with other consumerist trends. The shopping scene in China's larger cities has been enlivened in recent years by scores of privately run market stalls selling fashions from Canton (which have the cachet of being almost as stylish as designs from Hong Kong), denim jeans and high-heeled shoes.

Putting the finishing touches to his makeup, this leading Beijing opera actor prepares to play the Monkey King in Havoc in Heaven. *His virtuosity in this role has earned him the nickname 'Monkey'.* Havoc in Heaven *has a stirring plot which provides full scope for an actor to display his technical skills, be they in acrobatics, martial arts or singing. Generally an opera performer will have had some seven or eight years of basic training before he qualifies as a professional.*

In traditional Beijing opera, an actor is not concerned to express individual character. Instead he plays a role within the conventions laid down by precedent, and the elaborately painted faces are a part of this portrayal of role types. The audience knows that, for instance, a red-faced actor is brave and loyal and that a patch of white across the nose marks the character as a clown (right).

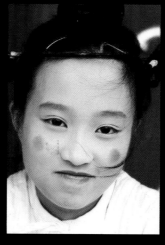

China's imperial past lived again in 1986 when Italian director Bernardo Bertolucci shot his epic The Last Emperor within the walls of the Forbidden City. This beautifully filmed extravaganza, which cost US$23 million to make, won nine of the 1988 Academy Awards. Four actors, including Tijer Tsou (right), played the part of Puyi, whose life spanned one of the most turbulent periods of Chinese history. The film documents Puyi's short-lived reign from the age of three, the ill-fated 'restoration' as puppet emperor of Manchukuo, and his final days as a simple gardener in Beijing.

Bernardo Bertolucci had the full co-operation of the Chinese Ministry of Radio, Television and Film to make The Last Emperor. The actors shown left were among the large cast recruited locally and from around the world.

Silks and satins glittered as the cast of The Last Emperor, *opulently dressed in the costumes of the Qing Dynasty, thronged the halls and gardens of imperial Beijing during location shooting. These ladies-in-waiting are taking a break in the grounds of the Summer Palace.*

Following page
*A view of the Forbidden City from the
north shows the symmetrical arrangement
of the palace halls.*